SAFARI ANIMALS

African Wildcat

Published by
Scholastic UK; Coventry, Warwickshire
Scholastic New Zealand Ltd; Greenmount, Auckland
Scholastic Australia Pty Ltd; Gosford NSW
Scholastic Canada Ltd; Markham, Ontario

Produced by Fog City Press,
a division of Weldon Owen Inc.
415 Jackson Street
San Francisco, CA 94111
www.weldonowen.com

Cover Design Bill Henderson
Text Maria Behan
Picture Research Brandi Valenza

Library of Congress Control Number is available by request

ISBN-13: 978-0-545-10070-0
ISBN-10: 0-545-10070-4

10 9 8 7 6 5 4 3 2 1

Color separations by San Choy International, Singapore.
Printed by Tien Wah Press in Singapore.

Warthog

What are safari animals? Well, a safari is a journey, so safari animals are ones that are so special, they're worth taking a trip to see.

The animals you'll find in this book are from Africa, and for many of us, Africa is very far away. But by turning the page, you can start out on your own safari—one where you'll meet some amazing animals!

On the plains
of Africa, animals
will often travel
in a group.
A group of zebras
is called a *herd*.

Zebras

Blesboks

Sometimes, you find an animal on its own, but most of the time, they stick together.

◀ Fish Eagle

White Rhinoceroses

Animals often hang out with their own kind. But sometimes, very different creatures team up, like hippos and birds.

Zebras

Wildebeest

Hippopotamuses and Egrets ▶

Meerkats

◀ *Hippopotamuses*

Guinea Fowl

Young animals learn from the other members of their families, just like we do.

Baby animals
usually stay close
to their mother.

Warthogs

African Elephant

It's good for young animals to explore a bit, though. It helps them pick up new skills...

◄ Lion Cub

Serval

Puku

...like flying, jumping, and roaring!

Secretary Bird

Lion ▶

Flamingos

Africa is home to many beautiful birds. This flock of pink flamingos looks like bright flowers blooming in the green grass.

Some African birds have red faces and striped wings, while others have head feathers that look like fancy hats!

Bateleur Eagle

Secretary Bird

Crowned Crane ▶

Black and White Colobus

What does this
leopard see way
up high? A bird?
Or maybe a
monkey?

◄ *Osprey*   *Leopard*

Or even a giraffe? Thanks to their l-o-n-g necks, giraffes are way up high even when they're standing on the ground!

Giraffe

Kudu

Some animals have large ears—so they can hear the things going on around them.

◄ Hare

African Wild Dog

Leopard

These animals have a great sense of sight, handy for hunting or just getting around in the dark. Here's looking at you, kid!

Bush Baby

Osprey ▶

Red Hartebeest

With other animals that live on the plains, horns are the feature that sticks out the most!

◀ *Kudu*

Nyala

Cheetahs are beautiful when they're at rest, but when they run, they are just a blur. Cheetahs are the fastest animal on Earth. They can run up to 75 miles per hour (120 kph)!

Cheetah

Rock Python

◄ *Serval*

Fish Eagle

Animals you might see on safari kill their prey in many ways: some with teeth, some with strangling hugs, and others with sharp talons!

With teeth like these, it's hard to believe this monkey mostly eats fruit!

Vervet Monkey

African Wild Dog

Animals that eat meat—like caracals, wild dogs, and hyenas—have strong teeth and jaws. The better to bite with!

◀ Caracal

Hyena

Gazelle

Other safari animals are gentle plant eaters, happiest when they have some tasty grass or berries to munch.

Blue Duiker

Defassa Waterbuck ▶

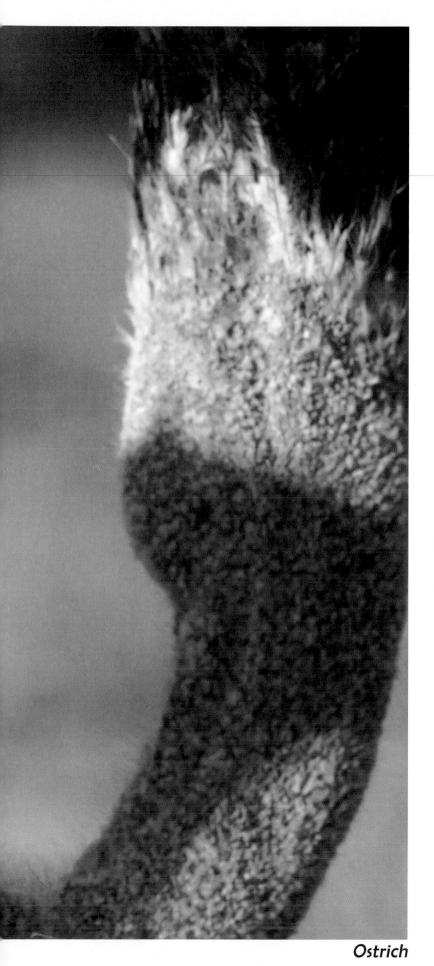

Ostriches eat creatures like bugs, but their favorite treats are nice, tasty leaves.

Ostrich

Animal meals are as different as the creatures eating them. But Mommy's tail isn't food—ouch!

Ground Squirrel

Crested Grebe

African Elephant ▶

Flamingos

Crocodile

Many African birds—and some creepier creatures—spend most of their time in or near the water.

◀ *Egret*

Hippos make splashing around in the water look like fun, don't they?

Hippopotamuses

Stork

Much of Africa is dry, so animals drink wherever they're lucky enough to find some water.

◀ *Giraffe*

Jackal

Bontebok

If people hunt them or move into their environment, these animals can get into trouble.

African Elephant ▶

Nile Monitor Lizard

Some animals that once were common across Africa now live in only a handful of places.

Warthog

◀ *Gorilla*

But if people work together, we can keep these wonderful animals part of our world for a long, long time!

Lion

African Wildcat
Africa and the Middle East

 Desert Warthog
Eastern and Southern Africa

 Chacma Baboon
Southern Africa

 Zebra
Eastern and Southern Africa

 African Fish Eagle
Sub-Saharan Africa

 Blesboks
South Africa

 White Rhinoceroses
South Africa

 Burchell's Zebras
Southern Africa

 Blue Wildebeest
Southern and East Africa

 Hippopotamuses and Egrets
Sub-Saharan Africa; worldwide except Antarctica

 Hippopotamuses
Sub-Saharan Africa

 Meerkat
Southern Africa

 Guinea Fowl
Africa

 Warthog
Eastern and Southern Africa

 African Lion Cub
Sub-Saharan Africa

 African Elephant
Sub-Saharan Africa

 Serval
Sub-Saharan Africa

 Puku
Central Southern Africa

 Secretary Bird
Sub-Saharan Africa

 African Lion
Sub-Saharan Africa

 Greater Flamingo
Africa, Southern Asia, Southern Europe

 Bateleur Eagle
Sub-Saharan Africa

 Secretary Bird
Sub-Saharan Africa

 Crowned Crane
Sub-Saharan Africa

 Osprey
Worldwide except Antarctica

 Black and White Colobus
East Africa

 Leopard
Sub-Saharan Africa

 Giraffe
Sub-Saharan Africa

 Hare
Africa

 Greater Kudu
Eastern and Southern Africa

 African Wild Dog
Eastern and Southern Africa

 Leopard
Sub-Saharan Africa

 Bush Baby
East and Sub-Saharan Africa

Osprey
Worldwide except Antarctica

Brown Hyena
Southern Africa

Hippopotamuses
Sub-Saharan Africa

Kudu
Africa

Grant's Gazelle
East Africa

Giraffe
Sub-Saharan Africa

Red Hartebeest
South Africa

Blue Duiker
Central and South Africa

Stork
Warm regions worldwide

Nyala
South Africa

Defassa Waterbuck
Western, Central, East, and Southern Africa

Black-backed Jackal
Southern and coastal East Africa

Cheetah
Africa

Ostrich
Africa

Bontebok
Southern Africa

Serval
Sub-Saharan Africa

Ground Squirrel
Worldwide except Antarctica

African Elephant
Sub-Saharan Africa

Rock Python
Sub-Saharan Africa

Crested Grebe
Europe, Asia, Africa, and Australia

Gorilla
African tropical and sub-tropical forests

African Fish Eagle
Sub-Saharan Africa

African Elephant
Sub-Saharan Africa

Nile Monitor Lizard
Africa

Vervet Monkey
South Africa

Egret
Worldwide except Antarctica

Warthog
Eastern and Southern Africa

Caracal
Africa, Western Asia

Lesser Flamingos
Africa, Pakistan, northwest India

African Lion
Sub-Saharan Africa

African Wild Dog
Eastern and Southern Africa

Nile Crocodile
Sub-Saharan Africa, Madagascar

Lesser Flamingo
Africa, Southern Asia

Flamingo

ACKNOWLEDGMENTS

Weldon Owen would like to thank the following people for their assistance in the production of this book: Karen Perez, Andreas Schueller, Heather Stewart, Sonia Vallabh, and Kevin Yuen.

IMAGE CREDITS

Key t=top; b=bottom; DT=Dreamstime; iSP=iStockphoto; SST=Shutterstock
2 SST; 5 SST; 6 SST; 9 SST; 10 DT; 11 t and b DT; 12 t iSP; 12 b DT; 13 SST; 14 SST; 15 t and b DT; 17 SST; 18 SST; 19 t SST; 19 b DT; 20 t and b DT; 21 SST; 22 SST; 24 t and b DT; 25 DT; 26 DT; 27 t and b DT; 29 DT; 30 SST; 31 t and b DT; 32 t and b DT; 33 DT; 34 DT; 35 t and b DT; 37 SST; 38 DT; 39 t DT; 39 b SST; 41 SST; 42 SST; 43 t and b SST; 44 t SST; 44 b DT; 45 SST; 46 SST; 48 t and b DT; 49 SST; 50 DT; 51 t and b DT; 53 SST; 54 DT; 55 t and b DT; 56 DT; 57 SST; 58 SST; 59 t and b DT; 61 SST; 64 DT.